KIDZBIZ

GAMES
and
TOYS

Gillian Souter

Off the Shelf Publishing

BEFORE YOU START...

It's always fun to have a new game to play. Here are lots of ideas for toys and games you can make using all sorts of bits and pieces. There are pictures to give you some ideas, but it's fun to make up your own designs and colour schemes.

Some of these projects can get a bit messy, so keep your work area clean and cover it with scrap paper before any painting. Use non-toxic paints such as acrylics or poster paints.

If you need to draw a circle, draw around a glass or another round object, or use a pair of compasses.

Ask for an adult's help if you need to use a craft knife or the kitchen oven.

First published in 2000 by
Off the Shelf Publishing
32 Thomas Street
Lewisham NSW 2049
Australia

Projects, text and layout
copyright © 2000 Off the Shelf Publishing
Line illustrations by Clare Watson
Photographs by Andre Martin

Contents

Useful Stuff

Most of the things you'll need for making games and toys can be found around the house.

It's useful to have different types of paper, thin card and cardboard. Save cereal boxes and greetings cards. Buy some bright sheets of paper and card.

A good set of felt pens will be useful for many of the projects in this book. Choose ones which wash out of clothing!

Bright squares of felt can be bought at craft shops. Keep small offcuts for future projects.

Drinking straws are used in several projects in this book. Collect ice cream sticks or buy a packet from a craft shop.

Keep cardboard rolls of all sizes, from toilet rolls, kitchen towels and mailing tubes. Empty matchboxes and plastic bottles are also useful.

Buttons, beads and beans all make ideal counters for board games.

5

Tops & Spinners

Make a collection of colourful tops and see how many you can set spinning at the same time!

1 Use a pencil and compass to draw a circle on some stiff card.

2 Carefully pierce a hole in the centre with the point of the compass. Cut out the card disc.

3 Decorate the disc with felt pens. Push a cocktail stick through the hole and stop two-thirds of the way through.

1 To make a spinner, draw a circle then rule lines to divide it into six equal segments.

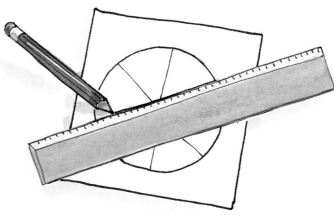

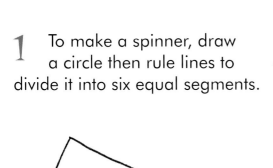

2 Join up these lines around the outside edge. Cut along the outside lines to make a hexagon. Then follow step 3.

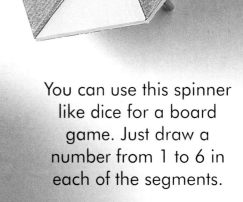

If you draw blue, yellow and red dots in a pattern like this, they will merge into bands when you spin the top.

You can use this spinner like dice for a board game. Just draw a number from 1 to 6 in each of the segments.

Remember This?

To make matching cards for
the game of memory, you will
need two identical brochures:
get them from a shop,
or ask friends next door
for their junk mail.

1 Cover one side of a sheet
of cardboard with some
adhesive covering or nice
wrapping paper. This will
be the back of the cards.

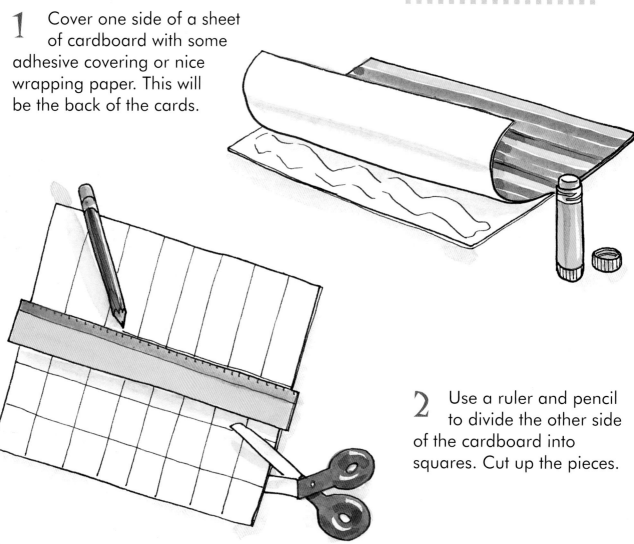

2 Use a ruler and pencil
to divide the other side
of the cardboard into
squares. Cut up the pieces.

3 Cut out pairs of interesting pictures from brochures, or draw your own pairs of pictures.

4 Glue each picture onto a card square. You can make as many pairs of cards as you like: the more cards, the harder the game.

To play: Lay all the cards face down. Players take turns to turn over two cards at a time. If they match, the player wins them and has another turn.

The winner is the player with the most cards at the end of the game.

Stacks o' Jacks

Make your own set of jacks with butterfly pasta or peanuts still in the shell.

YOU WILL NEED

pasta or peanuts
paints
a paint brush
felt
thread or wool
a needle

1 Paint pieces of pasta or peanuts in bright colours. Leave them to dry.

2 To make the bag, cut two rectangles of felt and lay them together. Thread a large needle with cotton or wool and knot the end.

3 Sew along one of the long edges as shown. Continue until three edges of the felt are stitched and then knot the thread.

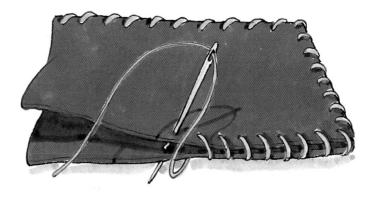

4 Make long stitches around the neck of the bag through one layer of felt only. Knot the ends at one side.

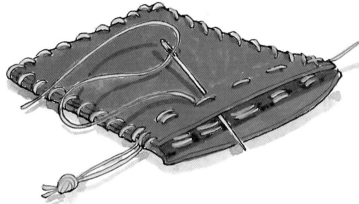

5 Thread the needle again and, starting at the opposite side, work back over your long stitches. Knot the ends; your bag now has two draw-strings.

To play: Toss six jacks and catch as many as possible on the back your hand, then toss these and catch them in your palm. Toss these and pick up one of the dropped jacks before catching. Repeat this until you've picked them all up. You'll improve with practice!

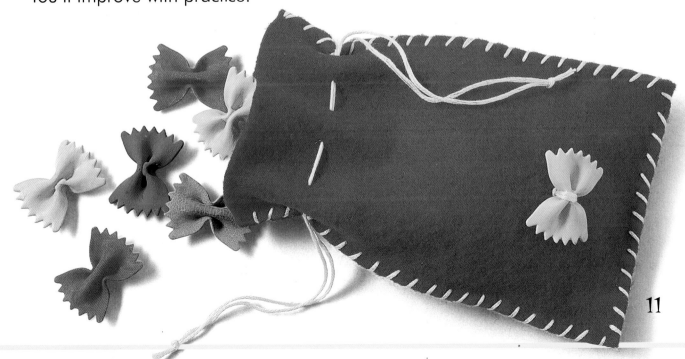

Pup-Pets

Scraps of felt are great for making finger puppets. You could make animals, people, or just weird things!

1 Draw or trace the basic design onto a piece of paper and cut it out to make your pattern.

2 Lay the pattern on some felt, draw around it with a felt pen and cut out the shape. Cut a front and back piece for each puppet.

3 Cut scraps of felt to make eyes, hair, noses, wings and other features. Arrange them until you are happy with the results.

4 Glue the features onto the front section. Glue any tails or wings on the other side of this section.

5 Spread a line of glue around the curved edge of the back section. Lay the front and back sections together and press flat.

Put a puppet on your index finger and make up a play for the cast to act out.

Fortune Teller

Amaze your friends by looking into the future and reading fortunes with this awesome device.

1 Fold each corner of your paper square into the centre to make a smaller square.

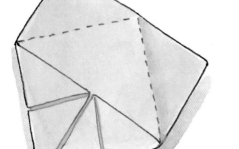

2 Turn the shape over and fold each corner into the centre again.

3 Mark each small triangle with a crayon dot in a different colour as shown.

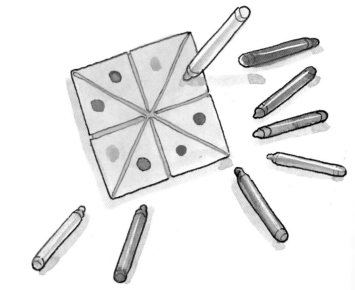

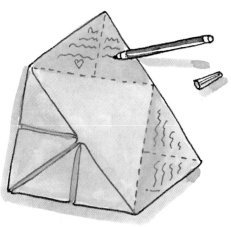

4 Lift each flap and write a silly fortune in half of the space underneath (such as "You will be the first human on Mars"). There is space for eight fortunes.

5 Turn the fortune teller over and write a number on each of the four flaps.

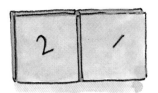

6 Fold it in half, unfold, then fold in half the other way. Now put your thumbs and forefingers behind each numbered flap.

To play: Ask a friend to choose a number. Move the fortune teller in and out while counting. Let your friend choose a colour and lift that flap to reveal the future!

Pick-up-sticks

You don't have to eat thirty ice-blocks - you can buy these sticks in craft shops!

YOU WILL NEED

ice-block sticks
paints
a paintbrush
a cardboard tube
stiff cardboard
a pencil
scissors
paper
glue

1 Decorate 30 or so clean ice-block sticks with bright paints or felt pens.

2 Cut a piece of cardboard tube shorter than the sticks. Glue a strip of paper around one end of the tube, so that it overlaps the rim.

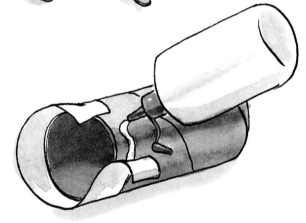

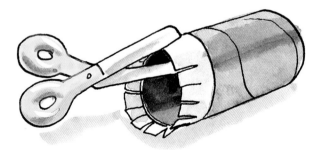

3 Make a series of snips into the paper, cutting right up to the cardboard tube.

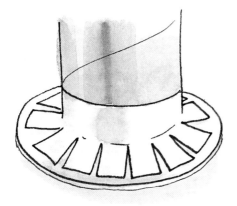

4 Fold the paper tabs out and glue them flat onto a cardboard disc that is bigger than the tube.

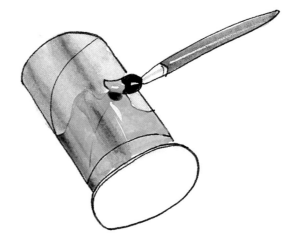

5 Paint both the tube and its base. When the paint is dry, you can add a coat of varnish.

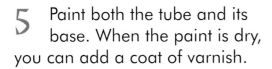

To play: Keep one 'lifter' stick and drop the others in a heap. The first player uses the lifter to remove one stick at a time. If any other sticks move, the lifter passes to the next player.

17

Parachutes

Make one each with
your friends and see
which parachute
lands last.

1 Make a small figure with
modelling clay and push a loop
of wire in the top. Ask an adult to
bake the model in the oven, following
the instructions on the packet.

2 Cut a square from a
plastic bag and use
a pen to push a small hole
near each corner.

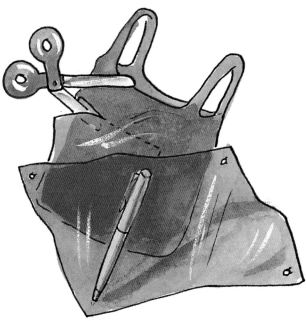

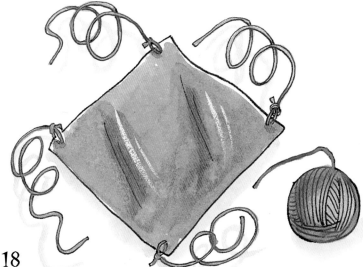

3 Cut four pieces of string
all the same length. Tie
one to each corner of the
plastic square.

18

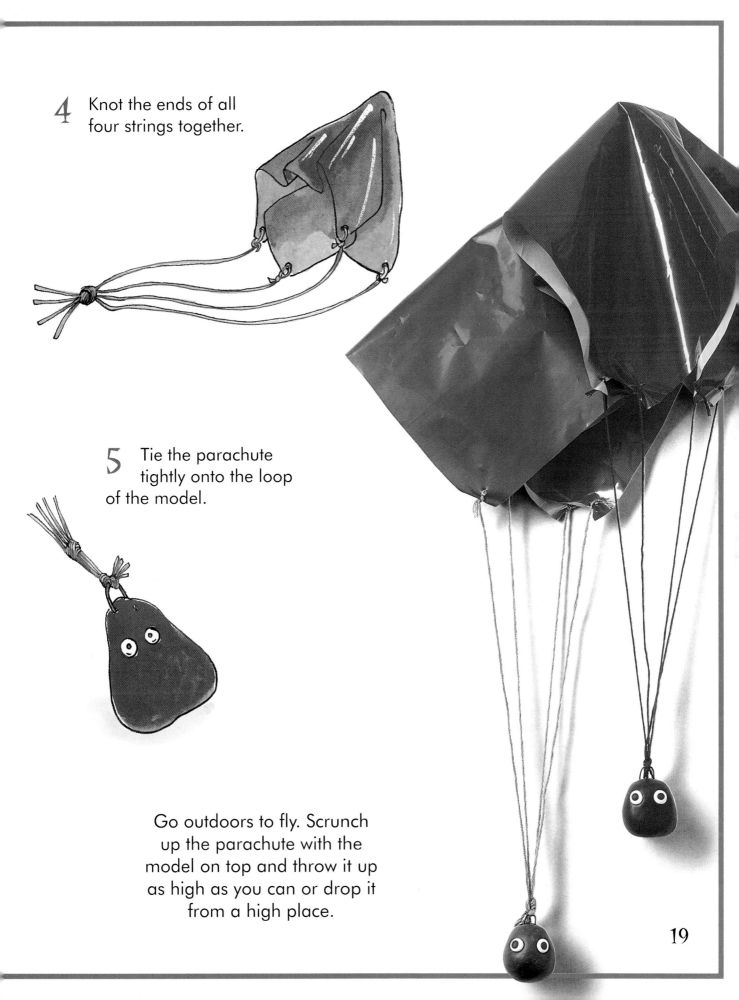

4 Knot the ends of all four strings together.

5 Tie the parachute tightly onto the loop of the model.

Go outdoors to fly. Scrunch up the parachute with the model on top and throw it up as high as you can or drop it from a high place.

Kaleidoscope

Everything you need to make this clever toy can be bought from a newsagent's shop.

1 Cut a cardboard tube 17 cm long. Cut another piece just 7 mm long. Line the inside of the long tube with a rolled rectangle of thin black card or paper.

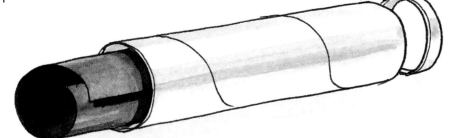

2 Cut a rectangle of acetate that is 17 cm long and about 2.5 times the diameter of the cardboard tube. Score two lines and fold it in three to make a triangular tube. Put this in the long cardboard tube.

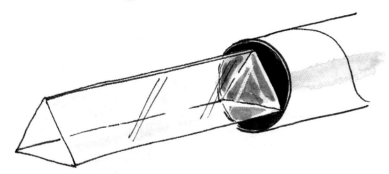

3 Cut a disc of cardboard to fit the tube. Poke a peep-hole in the centre and tape it onto one end of the long tube.

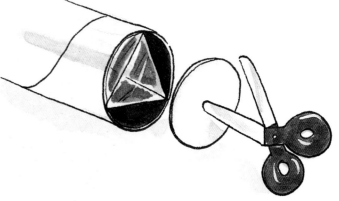

4 Cut two acetate discs the same diameter as the tube. Place one on the other end of the long tube, place the cardboard ring on top and tape the sections together.

5 Put a handful of beads, paper clips and other small shapes into the ring cavity and tape the other acetate disc over it.

6 Decorate your kaleidoscope with paint, felt pens or bright wrapping paper.

Point the tube towards a light and turn it to see the interesting patterns.

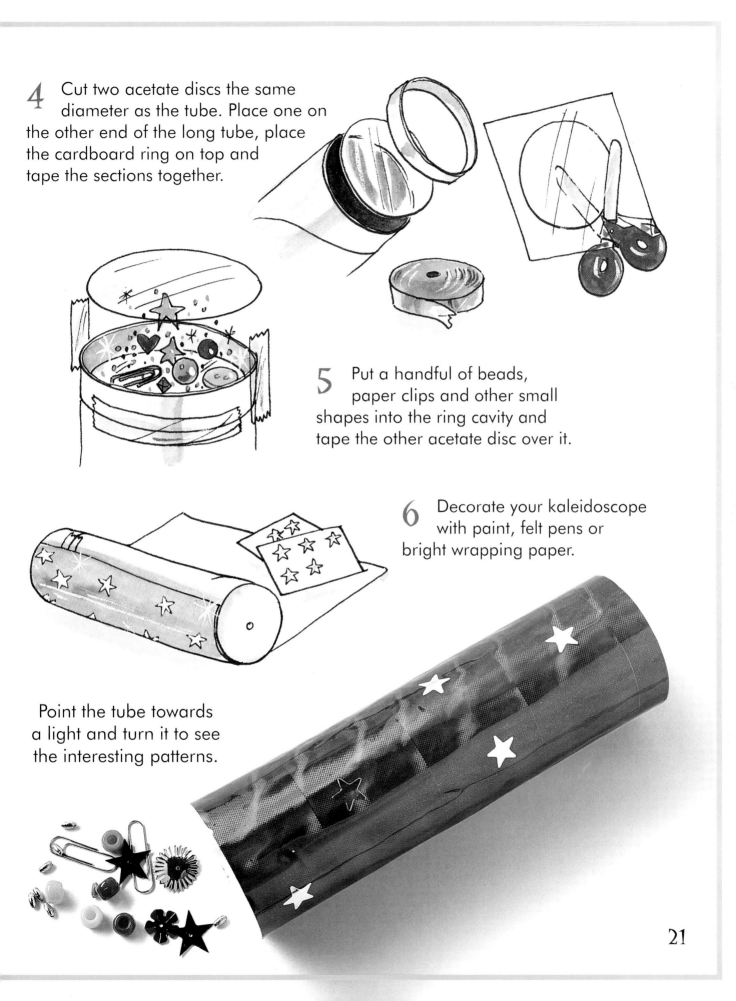

Boat Races

You don't need to be a
millionaire to enter
these boat races!

1 Find three corks the
same size and glue
them together to make
a raft.

2 Draw a curved triangle
on a sheet of acetate and
colour it with felt pens. When
it is dry, cut out the sail.

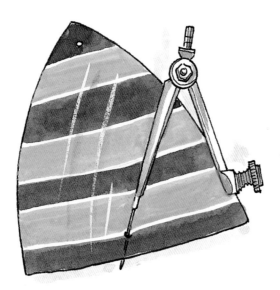

3 Use a large needle or the
point of a pair of compasses
to make a hole near the top and
bottom of the sail.

22

4 Push a wooden skewer through the two holes and into the middle cork. Cut the skewer above the sail if necessary.

5 Make small flags and stick them in lumps of plasticine. Arrange these in a large baking dish and half-fill it with water.

To play: Blow your boat around a water course with a straw. You could have two boats racing together, or you could time each boat as it completes the course separately.

23

Bead Boy

YOU WILL NEED

6 small beads
12 long beads
6 big round beads
hat elastic
scissors

String a bead boy and
jiggle the elastic to make
him dance.

1   On some hat elastic, thread a
    small bead, three long beads and
another small bead, then take the
elastic back through the long beads.

2   Now thread on two big
    round beads, three long
beads and a small bead, then
take the elastic back through
the long beads.

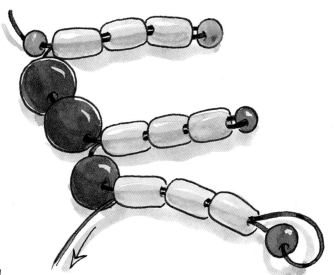

3   Now thread on one big
    round bead, three long
beads and a small bead, then
take the elastic back through
the long beads.

24

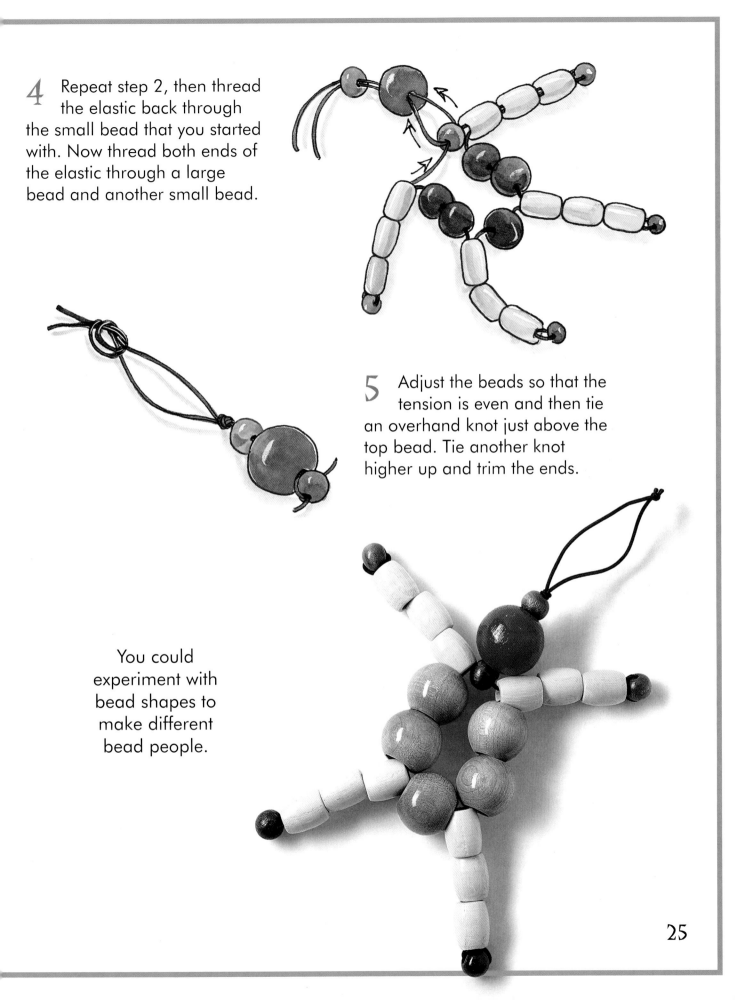

4   Repeat step 2, then thread the elastic back through the small bead that you started with. Now thread both ends of the elastic through a large bead and another small bead.

5   Adjust the beads so that the tension is even and then tie an overhand knot just above the top bead. Tie another knot higher up and trim the ends.

You could experiment with bead shapes to make different bead people.

25

Jugglers

The best time to learn to juggle is as soon as possible! Make three of these colourful jugglers and get a head start.

1 Cut felt into 5 cm squares. You will need six squares to make each juggler.

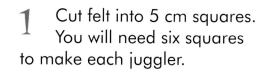

2 Thread a large needle and knot the end of the thread. Lay two felt squares together and stitch along one edge.

3 Stitch a new square onto the second edge of the first square. Continue this way until you have joined five squares together.

26

4 Stitch all the sides together to make a box. Stitch the sixth square on like a lid but leave a gap.

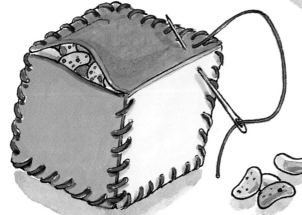

5 Fill the juggler with dry beans and stitch the gap closed.

To juggle three balls, throw them in a criss-cross pattern. Start with just one and practise tossing it from hand to hand - without watching your hands!

27

Shove-a-Coin

This old game was played with ha'pennies - you can play with any type of small coin.

1 Take the lid off an unwanted shoe box and cut the flap off one of the narrow ends.

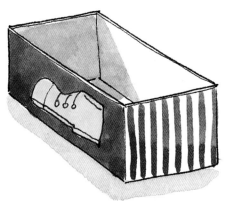

2 Use the base of the box to draw seven pencil lines across the inside of the lid. The distance between each line should be just a little more than the size of your small coin.

28

3 Leave the far end of the lid blank and colour in the other stripes with felt pens.

4 Cut a strip of cardboard for each player to keep their score. Colour these so that they match the stripes on your playing board.

To play: Place the coin at the edge of the board and hit it with a flat hand. Players must land the coin on each colour three times. Score by placing a counter on your card strip for each success.

29

Sticky Ball

You'll need one plate for each player for this catching game. You could use a sock ball instead of a polystyrene one.

YOU WILL NEED

picnic plates
a polystyrene ball
acrylic paints
a paintbrush
a craft knife
ribbon or cloth tape
strong glue
Velcro dots
a felt pen

1 Place your catching hand face down on a plastic or paper plate and mark either side of your hand. Ask an adult to cut two slots along the marks with a craft knife.

2 Thread wide ribbon or cloth tape through the slots to make a handle on the back of the plate. Check that your hand fits and then glue the ends onto the inside of the plate.

3 Stick Velcro dots (the scratchy side) over the ribbon ends and around the inside of the plate.

4 Paint a polystyrene ball. When it is dry, stick Velcro dots (the furry side) evenly around the ball.

Now, team up with a friend and try catching the furry ball with your sticky mitt.

Snap!

Here's a card game for two or three players. First, make your cards!

YOU WILL NEED

white card
a ruler
a pencil
scissors
a black pen
thick felt pens

1 On a large sheet of white card draw lots of shapes with felt pens. This will be the back of the cards.

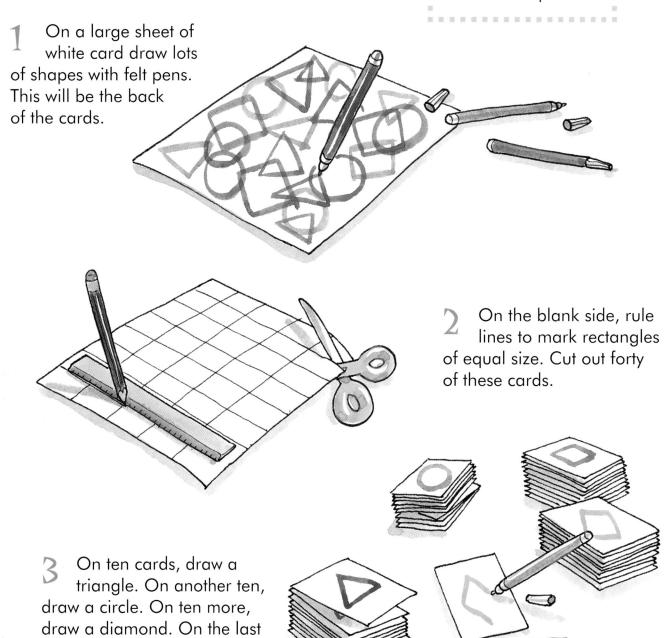

2 On the blank side, rule lines to mark rectangles of equal size. Cut out forty of these cards.

3 On ten cards, draw a triangle. On another ten, draw a circle. On ten more, draw a diamond. On the last ten, draw a square.

32

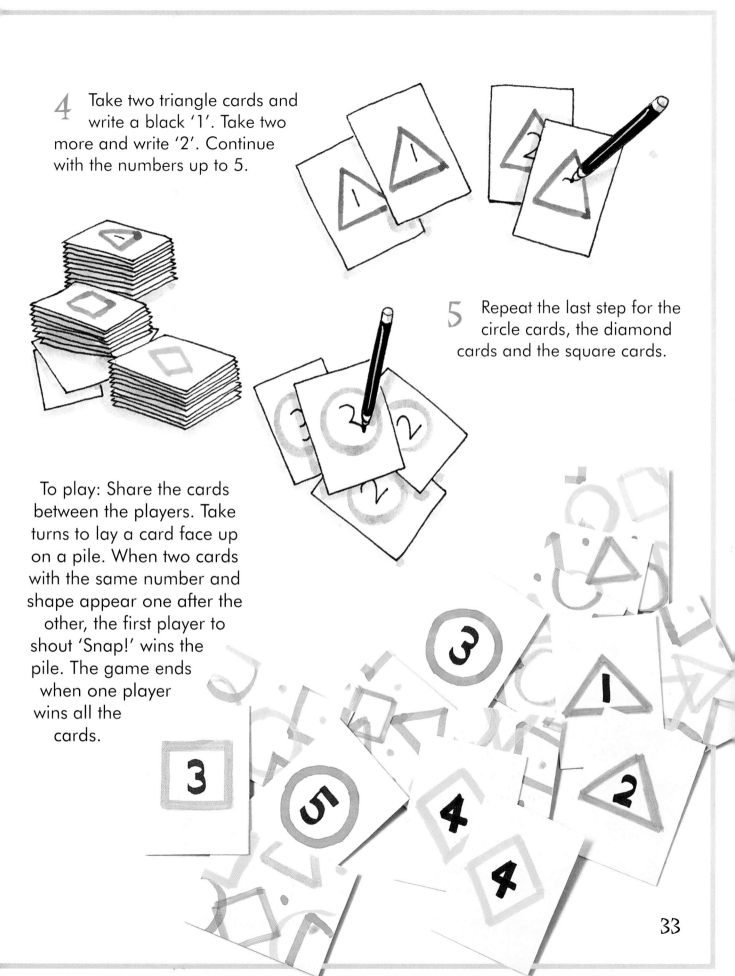

4 Take two triangle cards and write a black '1'. Take two more and write '2'. Continue with the numbers up to 5.

5 Repeat the last step for the circle cards, the diamond cards and the square cards.

To play: Share the cards between the players. Take turns to lay a card face up on a pile. When two cards with the same number and shape appear one after the other, the first player to shout 'Snap!' wins the pile. The game ends when one player wins all the cards.

33

Flying Trapeze

These high flyers will
risk everything to spin
for your delight.

YOU WILL NEED

tracing paper
a pencil
white cardboard
felt pens
scissors
glue & tape
a drinking straw
small coins
string

1 Trace over the pattern in pencil.
Lay the tracing face down on
thin card and draw over the lines.
Cut the card along the pencil
outline.

2 Repeat step 1 to
make a second
section. Colour both
sections with
felt pens.

3 On the back of one section,
glue a small coin at each
end. Cut a piece of straw and
glue it in the middle. Glue
the other section on top.

34

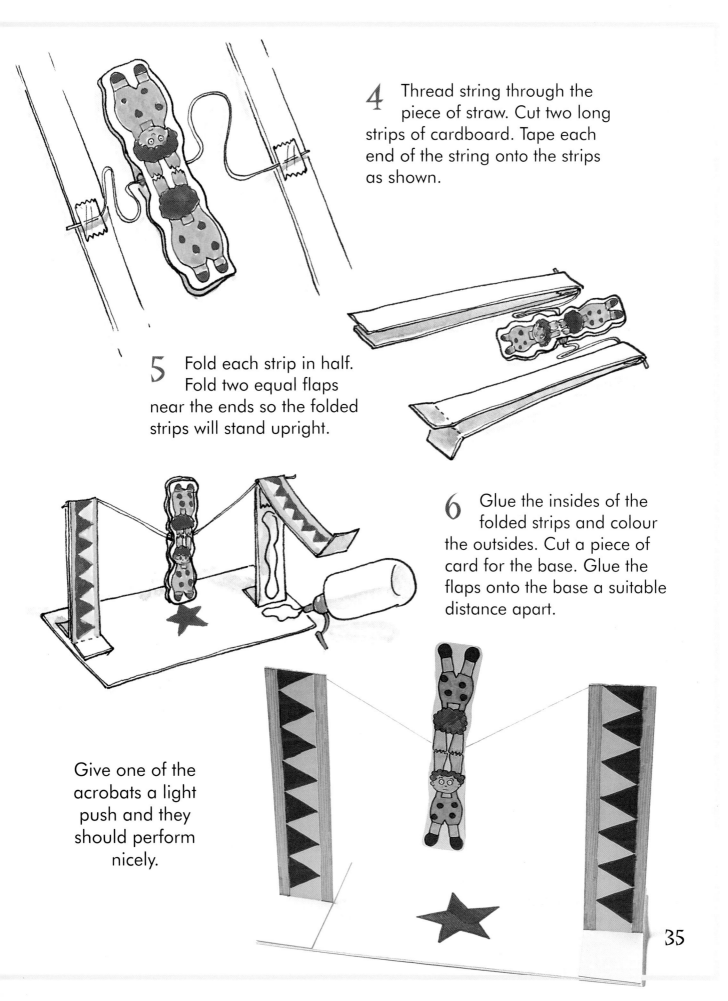

4   Thread string through the piece of straw. Cut two long strips of cardboard. Tape each end of the string onto the strips as shown.

5   Fold each strip in half. Fold two equal flaps near the ends so the folded strips will stand upright.

6   Glue the insides of the folded strips and colour the outsides. Cut a piece of card for the base. Glue the flaps onto the base a suitable distance apart.

Give one of the acrobats a light push and they should perform nicely.

Snakes & Ladders

Make your own board
for this classic game.
For a longer game, make
a board with sixty-four
squares.

1 Cut eighteen squares of
paper in one colour and
eighteen in another colour.

2 Arrange these in rows of
six in a checked pattern
on a sheet of stiff cardboard.
Paste each one in place.

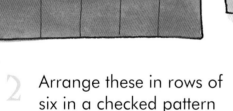

3 Starting at the bottom left
corner, number each square
from 1 to 36. At the end of each
row, work up and then along.

4 Cut pipe cleaners into different lengths and shape them into snakes. Twist one end to make a head and glue on paper eyes.

5 Cut two equal lengths of pipe cleaner and join them with several short pieces. Make more ladders of different lengths then arrange them with the snakes on the board.

6 Look in the index at the back to find the steps for making a spinner. Mark the segments of your spinner 1 to 6.

To play:
Take turns to spin and move a counter up the board. If you land at the bottom of a ladder, climb to the top. If you land on a snake head, you must slide down. The first to reach square 36 wins!

Whirligigs

Here are two types of flying toy that are quite easy to make.

YOU WILL NEED

cardboard & card
a pencil
a ruler
scissors
coloured paper
glue

1   Measure and cut a 20 x 2.5 cm strip of corrugated cardboard from a large box. Paint both sides or glue on some bright paper.

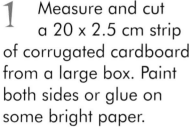

2   Round the corners of the propellor with your scissors. Carefully mark the centre point and then make a hole to fit the shaft tightly.

3   Glue a rectangle of paper around the pencil. Spread some glue near the sharp end of the pencil. Push it into the hole and allow the glue to dry.

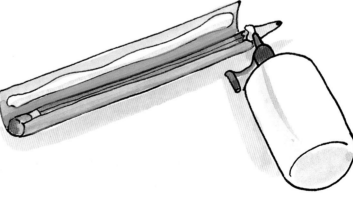

1   Measure and cut two 15 x 4 cm strips of thin card. Fold a 2.5 cm flap at the end of each strip.

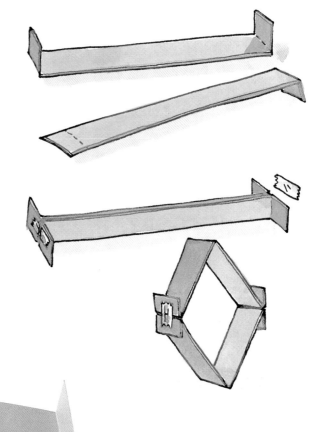

2   Lay the strips together and tape along the flaps to join the pieces. Push the flaps to the centre and crease the top and bottom to form a diamond.

Hold the diamond whirligig with two fingers on top and your thumb inside. Push with your fingers as you launch it so that it flips as it flies.

To fly the T-whirligig, twirl the pencil between the palms of your hands and let it go. Add a ball of plasticine on the tip for safety.

Skittles

Collect your plastic drink bottles to make a set of skittles.

1 Clean and dry the plastic bottles. Pour a few handfuls of dry sand into each bottle.

2 Crumple newspaper into a ball around the neck of a bottle. Cover the ball with a round piece of newspaper and gather the neck with a strip of masking tape.

3 Thin PVA glue by adding some water and brush this mixture over the newspaper. Paste a few strips of newspaper around the bottle and leave to dry.

40

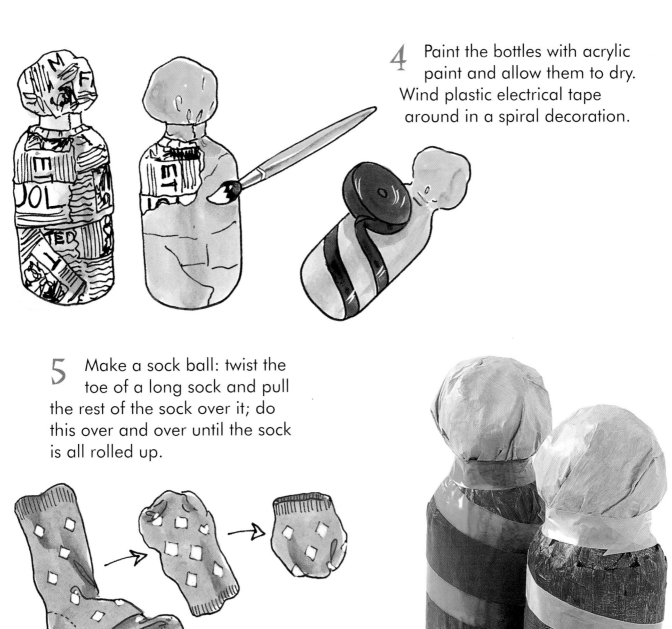

4 Paint the bottles with acrylic paint and allow them to dry. Wind plastic electrical tape around in a spiral decoration.

5 Make a sock ball: twist the toe of a long sock and pull the rest of the sock over it; do this over and over until the sock is all rolled up.

Set up the skittles in a group and see how many you can bowl over.

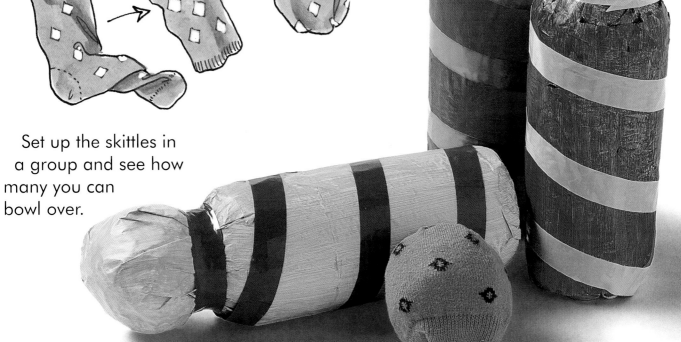

Buzzers

This simple spinning
toy makes a whizzing
noise and looks really
good in action.

YOU WILL NEED

a pencil
a large glass
stiff cardboard
scissors
a metal skewer
a hole punch
felt pens
wool

1 Lay an upturned glass
   on stiff cardboard
and draw around it
with a pencil.

2 Cut out the card-
   board circle with
a pair of scissors.

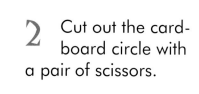

3 Decorate both sides of
   the buzzer with felt pens.
Use a hole punch to make
noise-making holes around
the rim.

42

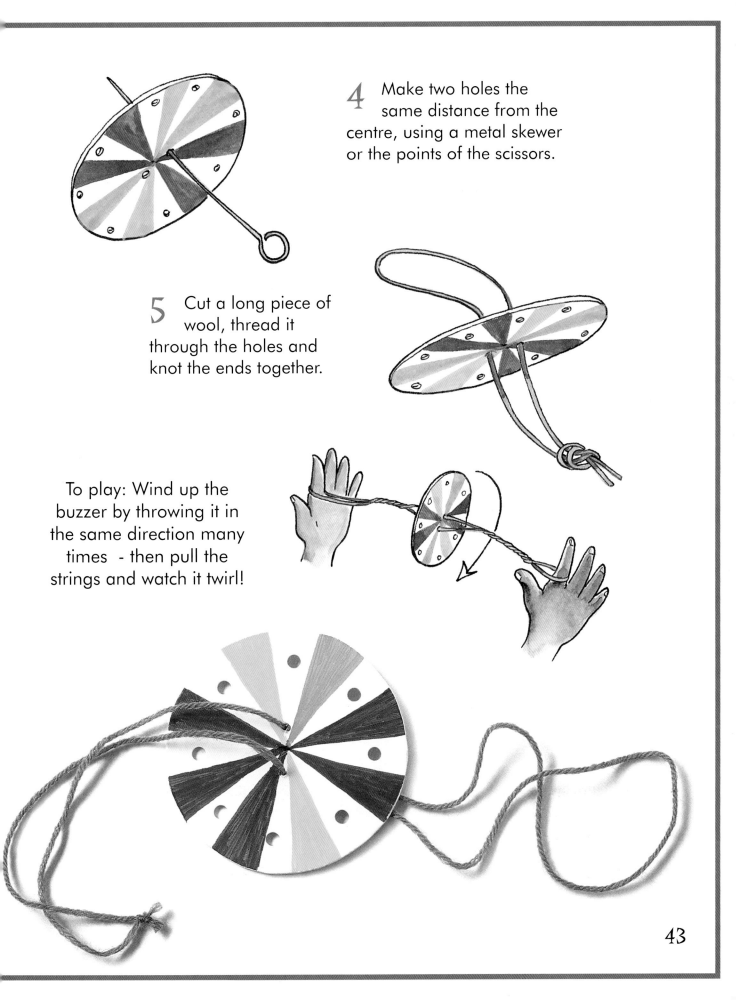

4 Make two holes the same distance from the centre, using a metal skewer or the points of the scissors.

5 Cut a long piece of wool, thread it through the holes and knot the ends together.

To play: Wind up the buzzer by throwing it in the same direction many times - then pull the strings and watch it twirl!

Blow Ball

Here's a great indoors game for two players. When you've finished, store all the parts away in a box for the next time you play.

1 Collect lots of cardboard tubes and matchboxes. Paint them or cover them with coloured paper.

2 Cut a piece of string or rope to fit around your table or desk and thread it through all the tubes.

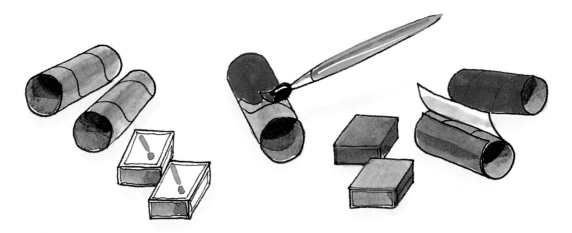

44

3 Knot the ends of the string together. Arrange this tube boundary around the table.

4 Glue four matchboxes together as shown to make a goal. Make another goal in the same way and set one at each end of the table.

To play: Place the ping-pong ball in the middle. Each player has a straw. Players cannot touch the ball and must try to score goals by blowing through the straw.

Beastie Twist

Mix some weird animals
with this device, which
needs a little extra care
and planning.

1 Cut 11.5 cm of cardboard tube.
Cut two 1-cm-wide strips of card
to fit around the tube and colour
them with a felt pen.

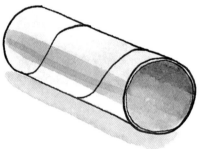

2 Cut a piece of paper
9 cm wide and 2 cm
longer than the narrow
strips. Fold it into six equal
panels.

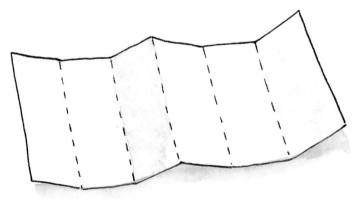

3 Check the fit of the paper
pattern around the tube: all
sides should touch and the ends
meet. Adjust the size if necessary.

46

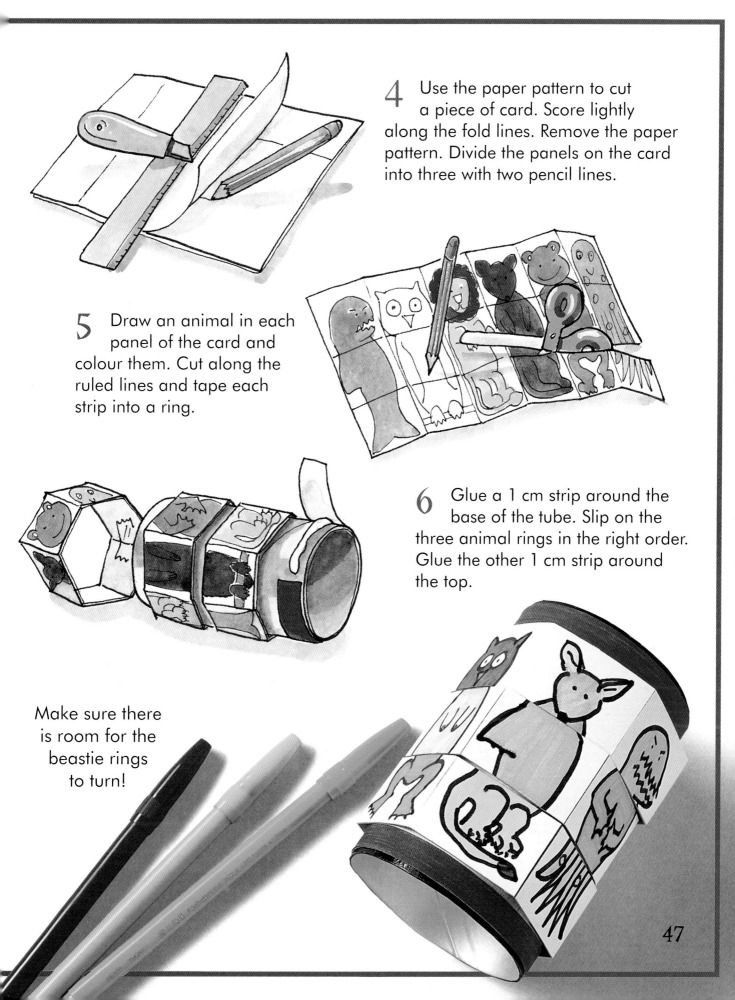

4 Use the paper pattern to cut a piece of card. Score lightly along the fold lines. Remove the paper pattern. Divide the panels on the card into three with two pencil lines.

5 Draw an animal in each panel of the card and colour them. Cut along the ruled lines and tape each strip into a ring.

6 Glue a 1 cm strip around the base of the tube. Slip on the three animal rings in the right order. Glue the other 1 cm strip around the top.

Make sure there is room for the beastie rings to turn!

Index